Not Afraid to Love

Matthew Bennett

Presentation by *BookLeaf Publishing*

Web: www.bookleafpub.com

E-mail: info@bookleafpub.com

ISBN: 978-93-95755-35-1

First edition 2022

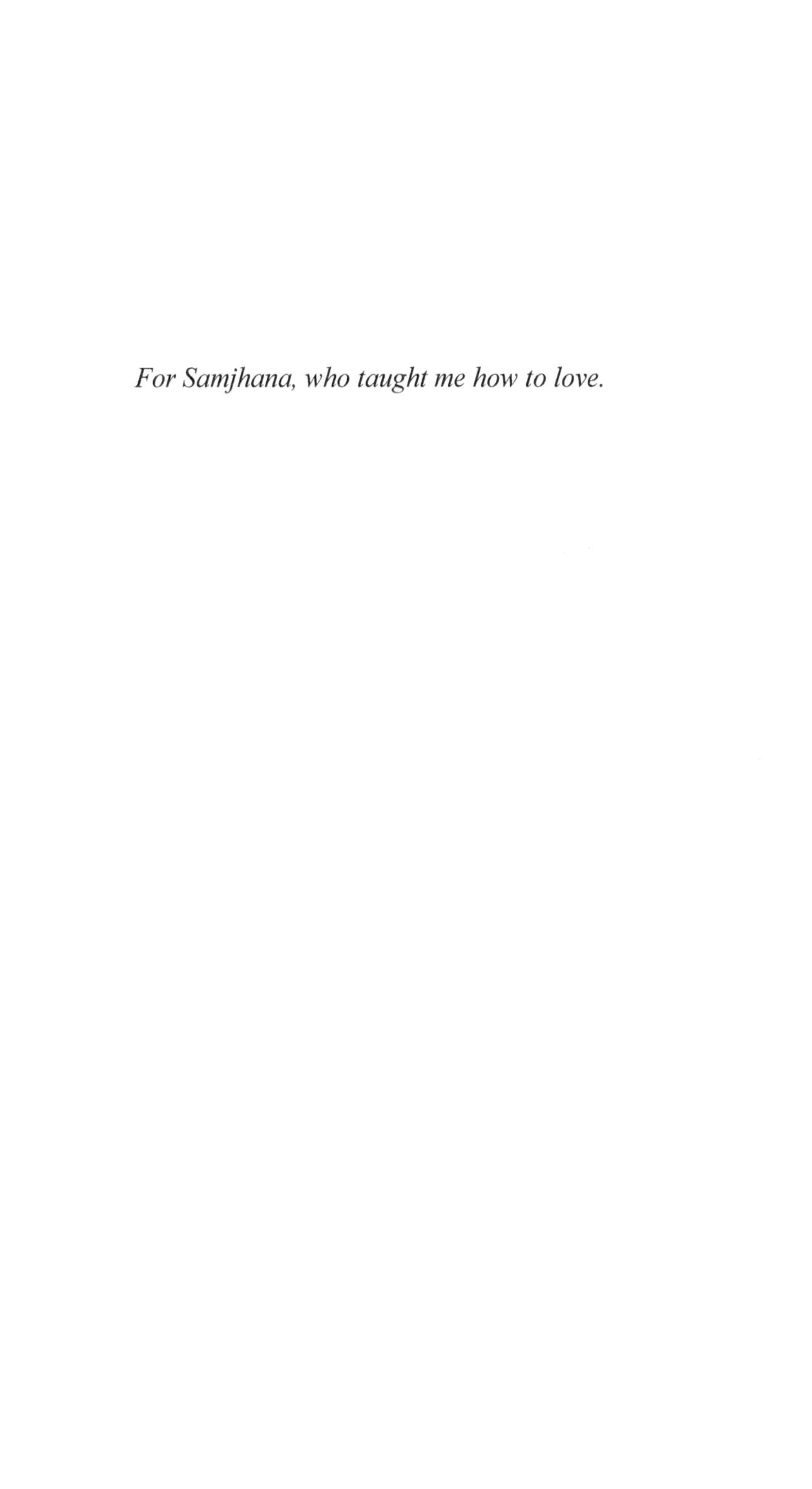

For Samjhana, who taught me how to love.

PREFACE

Everything written in this book is based on my life, the way I felt through different stages of growing up. The relationships over the years have taught me lessons that have helped to shape the future version of me. My book is intended mainly for my self serving reflections, inspired by the poetic love of my life. Hope she reads this and gets to learn a little more about my journey.

Lessons from my Father

I learned a lot from you growing up.
Such valuable lessons that have shaped my
whole life.
Yet these were not the lessons a Father should
teach his Son.

You taught me how to break a family,
how to let down those you love most.
You taught me how to run, to be a coward.
You taught me how selfish you really are.

I never did learn to shave, to put up a shelf
I didn't learn to fix things.
I guess these are years I'll never get back,
Always playing catch up.
Not ready for the world.

But you later showed me that I could forgive,
That I have empathy for those that fuck up.
You showed me there are two sides to every
story,
How easy it can be to make mistakes.

The thing is, you did teach me a lot.
Lessons more valuable than you could have
intended.

You taught me that the person I want to be is the opposite of the person you became.
You taught me what not to do.
Lessons I am thankful I didn't have to learn for myself.

Thank you for that.

A Mothers Love

I can't imagine bringing up a family without the
support you deserved.
I can't imagine your sacrifice, what you gave up
for us.
You struggled through year after year,
Thinking you couldn't give us enough.

You gave us everything and more,
You helped me become the person I am.
Despite the odds, I do believe in love.
I am empathatic, I care, I want the best for those
around me.
I learned to love hopelessly,
To give my whole heart.
I'm not afraid to love despite my share of breaks.
Your determination to keep going gives me
strength to go again.

Time heals all and lessons are there to be made.
But through it all, you showed me one thing
above all else.
To love, hopelessly.

Prior Engagements

I find it hard to remember my life from before.
To be young, unsure of anything.
To find myself in situations out of comfort.

I somehow drifted through ten years of life.
Barley thinking at all,
Day dreaming my way through each day.
Did I never stop to think for even one moment?
Life just wasting away.

I guess I never knew what I wanted.
From love, work, life itself.
A passenger in my own story.
Perhaps I was taunted by imaginary chants,
"You're just like your father"
But the honest truth is I didn't start living.
Simply existing.
I didn't think I deserved more.
Not wanting to let anyone down,
Somehow more important.

The engagement hanging over me,
It's the "right" thing to do.
Only then did I finally wake up.

I didn't know at the time what I wanted from
life,
I knew then what I didn't.

The truth is this time I'm not even sorry,
I have no regret.
Leaving you meant putting myself first,
I hadn't experienced that yet.

Caught in the Moment

It's tough to put into words why I followed you,
At the time I didn't put much thought into it.
To call it a rebound would be unfair,
Although I hadn't known you long.

For my loved ones at the time,
What must I be thinking?
I don't think I was thinking much at all.
Letting life just happen to me once more.

In an attempt to not lose what I had found,
I had lost what I had always desired.
I had so many reasons to stay for,
One reason to leave.
The hopeless romantic inside chose the latter.
I jumped in with all I had, not afraid to love.

I had some beautiful memories in the years to
follow,
but always tainted by loneliness.
Putting everything on one person,
When we had nobody else.
I always blamed her for me giving up so much,
Failed to get praise for my sacrifice.

I will always be thankful for these years,
My comfort zones stripped away.
I had to learn a lot about myself.
At times myself is all I really had,
Until I truly had nothing else.
Alone again.

The Darkest Year

The worst year of my life,
But also the most crucial.
Completely alone, for the first time.
To deal with myself, stuck in my head,
No way out.

Saying goodbye to my best friend,
Yet never saying much at all.
Still sharing four walls.
Waiting.
Painfully waiting for whatever happens next.

I look back and thank fuck you were still there
in some way.
I doubt I would have made it through,
Three days in particular.
Someone to cry on,
Someone to keep me safe from harm.
Looking back you helped me through,
Even in your silence.

A Man's Best Friends

I'll never forget my fluffy friends,
My two most beautiful girls.
Loki and Luna,
The troublesome twosome.
Who knew they could claim such a piece of my
heart.
Memories I'll always cherish.

You were there for me in my darkest hours,
You saved me with your love.
You loved me when I had nothing else,
Made me smile on my worst days.

I would do anything to hold you again,
For my path to cross again with yours.
You bought me all the joy in the world,
You also broke my heart when you went away.
When I lost, I lost it all.

I would kill to hold you once more,
But not sure I could suffer another goodbye.
I suffer without you nonetheless.

My babies, my besties, my little girls.
It's true what they say, I get it now.

"A dog is a man's best friend",
I was lucky enough to have two.

I'll never forget you both my darlings,
A love like no other.
Your names will always be with me,
Etched on my heart forever.

Wishing Well

Always wanting time away from others,
The loner is finally alone.
Time by myself I now have in excess,
More than I could possibly spend.
Be careful what you wish for.

A year spent in my own company,
Every single moment.
Every single day.

I always craved this time alone,
Time to recharge.
An escape from the world.

But of all my wishes to come true,
Why this one, why now?
Be more careful what you wish for,
For I have wasted one for sure.

Now my wishes are no longer wasted,
Saved for the most beautiful things.
Yet now that one was granted,
The rest are coming true.
Now I only wish for you.

Home Away from Home

The excitement of the trip home.
Three years apart.
Friends, family, familiarity, comfort,
Everything I had missed.

Pandemics steal from us all,
A debt never repaid.
Freedoms finally returned at last,
The perfect cure in sight.
It's time, I'm coming home,
At least I thought this at the time.

The thing is, I'm no longer alone.
Somehow in the chaos,
I've found my home away from home.
Right in front of me all along.

Five weeks "home" became five weeks of pain,
Away from my heart, my love.
The longest five weeks I could imagine.

Learning now that joy is hard to come by,
When not shared with the one you love.
Does it serve any purpose,
If making memories all alone?

Absence makes the heart grow fonder,
A tale as old as time itself.
Home really is where the heart is,
Unoriginal as it may sound.

You are my heart.
You are my home.

On the Bright Path

For all I have learned to this point,
I now put it into practise.
Finally on the path that's right,
Finally one that looks so bright.
For the first time in my whole life,
I see forever in my sights.
I see it clearly at last.

Thirty years in my pursuit of you,
Perfectly on time.
I had to find my way to you,
To be exactly here, exactly now,
To meet you in my prime.

A million insignificant choices,
Landed me right here you see,
Is there such a thing as freewill?
Or was this simply meant to be?

All I know is I have found you now,
Right as you have found me.
You were meant to be my Lady,
I was born to be your Lord.

Forever thankful for your love,
Love I have never felt before.

My First Letter to You

I'm going to miss you these next six days.

How will I make it through? I'm hopeless.
A few short weeks and I'm hooked on you.
The next date is all I want, to see you again.
Every moment you are on my mind.

You are unbelievable in a million ways.
Oh, I'm in trouble with this one!
Uranus, is my favourite spark in the sky.

My lady. MY lady.
You are ridiculously beautiful in every way.

Lady to your Lord,
A moment with you is worth a lifetime alone.
Dreams can come true, who knew?
You are the one I want.

I knew it then, I know it now.
Six days away was unbearable.
Six weeks was even worse.
We can get through it all together,
For that I know for sure.
Letters for you I will always write,
I will love you this way forever.

All These Things I Hate(d)

All these things I hate revolve around me.
This was how I wasted so many years,
Things about me I couldn't stand ,
So many of my fears.

The thing about being young is,
At the time it feels so real.
But as time goes on you realise,
It's not really how you feel.

For nothing I "hate" about mysel,f
Has ever caused a problem.
The fucking expectations put on us,
But yet, some think I'm awesome.

As I grow older I finally realise,
To put these feelings on a shelf.
How can you love anyone,
If you can't even love yourself.

The battle isn't over yet,
It's only just begun.
This journey is much easier when,
You've finally met the one.

For the one that loves me hopelessly,
Time to forget this pointless stuff.
The only thing that matters now,
I finally feel good enough.

The Taste of You

I've waited my whole life
To taste something this sweet.
My head between your legs again,
I would bow down at your feet.
Just to get a taste of you,
Just for one more chance,
I crave you every single day,
My life you just enhance.

Your taste is forever on my lips,
Fuck me, you taste so fine.
I always mean it when I say,
Baby, will you be mine?

The taste of lust, the taste of love,
The taste of you sat up above,
My face is where you do belong,
Your body fits mine just like a glove.

I do believe you were made for me,
You know I love you so much baby.
I always will. I swear this is true.
Now sit on my face, my fucking lady.

Stuck Inside my Head

No matter where you go in life,
You'll always be yourself.
Travel the world, find who you are,
Guess what - you're full of shit.
How can someone find something,
You've never even lost.

No escape from this stupid head,
My own worst enemy at times.
At times I want to run away,
But there I always am.

I wake up, I'm there.
I fall sleep, I'm there.
Today I'm here,
Tomorrow I'm here,
Just leave me the hell alone.

Just one day to be someone else,
Is all I ever ask.

My Better Half

Forever in your shadow,
Always looking up to you.
Not out of respect or admiration,
You're just so fucking tall.

All my silly jokes aside,
You're for sure my better half.
It's a shame you'll never see it,
You'll think I'm having a laugh.

But I mean it when I say
I'd do anything for you.
I'd give you a damn kidney,
Hell, I'd even give you two.

If you don't know it by now,
You surely never will.
I will love you until my dying breath,
Whoever hurts you I would kill.

Even when we are apart,
It doesn't bring me down.
You're my brother, my twin, my family
I love you with all I am.

I want great things for you,
Fuck, you deserve the world.
I wish I could give you everything.
I wish I could take away your worry.
I wish I could take away your pain.
I hope you know in your heart,
I would take it from you if I could.

There's a few people in this world,
The very best of the best.
Selfless, caring, pure of heart,
One thing I shall confess.

You are a pain in the arse.
I love you.

Other Brothers

I was never blessed with popularity,
I struggled through those early years.
Through childhood I was never seen,
Hiding in the shadows.
Never bullied, somehow worse,
I didn't exist, this was my curse.

As a young man, at fucking last,
I found my people, I loved you fast.
The best years of friendship,
Making up for lost time.
No matter where I am,
You're always in my heart

Leaving you both my biggest regrets.
How could I ever leave you, how?
You will always be with me yet,
I hate that I'm not with you now.

To call you best friends would be an insult.
Your love for me I could never fault.
You're my brothers by choice.
You're my brothers for life.

The Love of My Life

When time stops making sense,
When you know someone before meeting them.
When you find your purpose in another,
When you fall in love with one look.

I don't know much in this life
But I know one thing for sure,
When you know, you know.

My love for you I will always show.
Wherever you go, I will go.
My heart belongs at last,
I love you, this you know.

Night Owl

Not quite nocturnal,
Yet I live during the night.
Always found peace in the quiet hours,
Before the busy, before the bright.
I sit here in the darkness,
I could sit here all night.

Life has gone to bed,
I have come alive.
Nothing like having some time to kill,
I need it to survive.

The day quite often drains me,
I struggle to make it through.
Silly little night owl,
Time to recharge, to feel brand new.

A Hopeful Hopeless Romantic

I always believed in romance,
Never felt it for myself.
It's something saved for the films,
Something for the bookshelf.

But then came you,
Gifting me your book.
I cherish this for always,
The time you took,
To write your poetic words,
To share them with me.

You inspired me to write this in return,
Perhaps you'll learn the me before you.
I've never taken the time to think this through,
To look back on life, to speak my truth.

You bring out this side of me,
A side that wants to express.
By now you know me plenty,
I'm not trying to impress.
I just want you to know me,
To love me for who I am.

15/4/22

Strangers in Lidcome,
Meet for the first time.
A first date which was perfect,
A lady looking fine.

I'll never forget the day we shared,
It all just fell in place.
A walk I will always remember,
A first real look at that face.

Started out early and followed by dinner,
Yet too busy to date.
I don't question good things in my life,
This time it must be fate.

When my hope was all but gone,
You appeared at the right time.
Right then I knew why I was here,
Why life took the way of mine.

Sat under the stars, not a cloud in the sky.
I don't want this night to be through.
When will I see this lady again?
Funnily enough the next day,
K.G.F: Chapter 2.

Next to You

I have found my favourite thing in life,
Waking up next to you.
I could never ask for more,
Well, perhaps I wish you didn't snore.

You may be a real pain in my arse,
But I love you each and every day
I love you like our love is new.
No matter what life throws our way,
I'll always be next to you.

I know I'm not perfect,
I know you are not too.
But guess what little miss?
I want to wake up next to you.

No matter what you ever say,
No matter what you do.
Baby please don't worry,
I'll always be right here,
Right next to you.

100 Reasons Why

Why do I love you so?
You ask me all the time.
Yet when I think of one or two,
A hundred reasons come to mind.

Without hesitation,
Without pause.
I love you for countless reasons,
Not just because.

You asked me to list a hundred reasons,
I could list a thousand more.
You are my whole world,
Today and always.
I love you more than Jane loves Thor.

All my hopes are finally true,
My worries are all through.
You are my lady forever more,
I think I always knew.

The day I met you, I hoped it true.
Never been more sure.
The first time I told you I loved you,
My head between your..